YIN-YANG ZEN

Yin and Yang are one vital force...the primordial aura. ~ *Wang Yangming*

❧34 CREATIVE DESIGNS FOR RIGHT AND LEFT HAND COLORING❧

ALTHOUGH THE PAPER USED HEREIN IS OF HIGHER QUALITY STOCK, WE WANTED TO ENSURE THERE WOULD BE NO BLEED THROUGH BY FELT PENS AND/OR MARKERS. ACCORDINGLY, AN EXTRA PAGE HAS BEEN INSERTED IN BETWEEN EACH IMAGE.

PLEASE NOTE: This is not a children's coloring book.
Some images are intricately detailed and will require 100% of your attention.

All rights reserved. No part of this book may be reproduced in any form, or by any electronic means, including information storage and retrieval systems, without permission in writing from the publisher.

Copyright © 2017 Dawné Dominique
ISBN: 978-1-7750442-5-3
Cover and Art Designed by Dawné Dominique
Vector Copyrights © VectorStock & DepositPhotos

Published by DusktilDawn Publications
www.dusktildawndesigns.com
CANADA

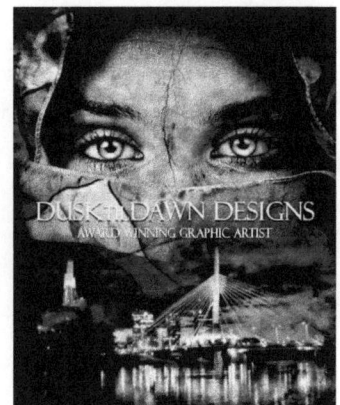

DUSKtilDAWN DESIGNS
AWARD WINNING GRAPHIC ARTIST

COLOR TESTING

COLOR TESTING

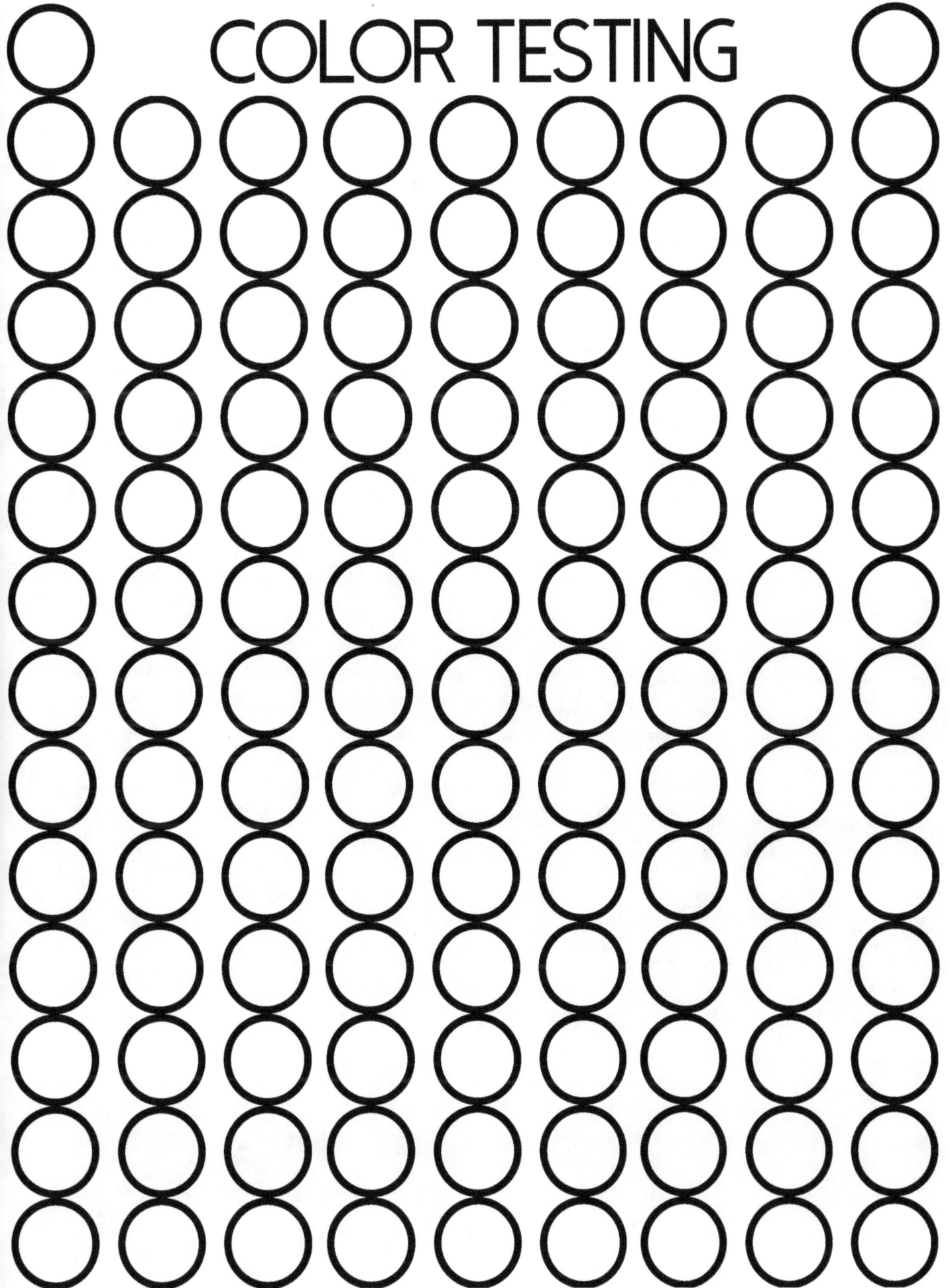

IF YOU ENJOYED THIS COLORING BOOK, DON'T BE SHY...LEAVE A REVIEW.

And check out other adult coloring books By Dawné Dominique & D. Thomas-Jerlo

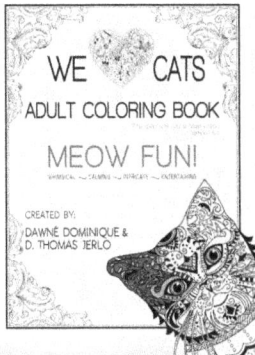

DAY OF THE DEAD TIRED
RELAX WITH A COLORING BOOK THAT MATCHES YOUR MOOD
CREATED BY:
DAWNÉ DOMINIQUE & D. THOMAS JERLO

WE ♥ CATS ADULT COLORING BOOK
MEOW FUN!
CREATED BY:
DAWNÉ DOMINIQUE & D. THOMAS JERLO

Zenology
AN *INTRICATE* ADULT COLORING BOOK
FIND YOUR HAPPY "ZEN" PLACE
CREATED BY:
DAWNÉ DOMINIQUE & D. THOMAS JERLO

FLOWER POWER ADULT COLORING BOOK
44 PAGES OF CREATIVE DESIGNS
BRINGING THE GARDEN TO YOU ONE BUD AT A TIME
CREATED BY:
DAWNÉ DOMINIQUE D. THOMAS JERLO

JEANETTE DeCOFF'S Dragonfly Kisses FAMILY COLORING BOOK
ALL PROCEEDS DONATED TO BREAST CANCER RESEARCH
CREATED BY:
DAWNE DOMINIQUE D THOMAS JERLO

www.lulu.com/spotlight/dusktildawn

Also available at:

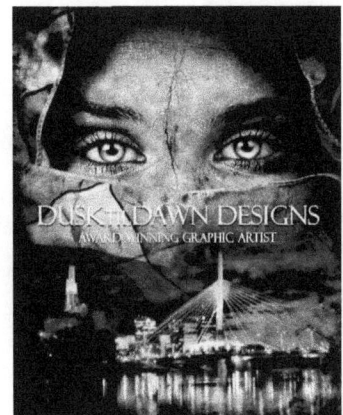

DUSKTILDAWN DESIGNS
AWARD WINNING GRAPHIC ARTIST

www.dusktildawndesigns.com

www.ingramcontent.com/pod-product-compliance
Lightning Source LLC
Chambersburg PA
CBHW081152090426
42736CB00017B/3283

* 9 7 8 1 7 7 5 0 4 4 2 5 3 *